D0845682

MAINE COON CATS

KATIE LAJINESS

Big Buddy Books
An Imprint of Abdo Publishing
abdopublishing.com

BIG BUDDY CATS

abdopublishing.com

Published by Abdo Publishing, a division of ABDO, PO Box 398166, Minneapolis, Minnesota 55439.
Copyright © 2018 by Abdo Consulting Group, Inc. International copyrights reserved in all countries.
No part of this book may be reproduced in any form without written permission from the publisher.
Big Buddy Books™ is a trademark and logo of Abdo Publishing.

Printed in the United States of America, North Mankato, Minnesota.
092017
012018

Cover Photo: Getty Images.
Interior Photos: ASSOCIATED PRESS (p. 17); depositphotos (p. 19); Getty Images (pp. 5, 7, 9, 11, 13, 15, 21, 23, 25, 27, 29, 30).

Coordinating Series Editor: Tamara L. Britton
Contributing Editor: Jill Roesler
Graphic Design: Jenny Christensen

Publisher's Cataloging-in-Publication Data

Names: Lajiness, Katie, author.
Title: Maine coon cats / by Katie Lajiness.
Description: Minneapolis, Minnesota : Abdo Publishing, 2018. | Series: Big buddy cats |
    Includes online resources and index.
Identifiers: LCCN 2017943907 | ISBN 9781532111990 (lib.bdg.) | ISBN 9781614799061 (ebook)
Subjects: LCSH: Maine coon cat--Juvenile literature. | Cats--Juvenile literature.
Classification: DDC 636.83--dc23
LC record available at https://lccn.loc.gov/2017943907

CONTENTS

A POPULAR BREED

Cats are popular pets. About 35 percent of US households have a cat. And, Americans own more than 85 million!

Around the world, there are more than 40 **domestic cat breeds**. One of these is the Maine coon cat. Let's learn why the Maine coon is the fifth-most popular cat breed in the United States.

Maine coons are larger than many domestic cat breeds. They are also calm creatures. So, many people call them gentle giants.

THE CAT FAMILY

All cats belong to the **Felidae** family. There are 37 **species** in this family. **Domestic cats** are part of one species. Lions and other types of cats make up the others.

Did you know?

Humans and cats have lived together for at least 3,500 years.

Brushing a Maine coon helps prevent knotted fur.

MAINE COON CATS

Some say Maine coons came to modern-day North America on **Viking** ships. Others believe the cats arrived on the boats of European sailors.

No matter how they arrived, some cats escaped from the boats. So, they had to live alone in the wild. Those with the thickest fur stayed warm during the New England winters. These were the first Maine coon cats.

The Maine coon is the official cat of the state of Maine.

Over hundreds of years, the Maine coon became the most popular cat in America. In 1878, the **breed** appeared in its first cat show in Boston, Massachusetts. And, the breed won Best in Show at an 1895 cat show.

By the 1950s, there were few Maine coons left. Other breeds had simply become more popular. But those who loved the Maine coon kept the breed alive. In 1976, the **Cat Fanciers' Association** fully recognized the Maine coon cat.

Long ago, many Maine coons were born with extra toes. Today, it is rare for a Maine coon to have extra toes.

WHAT THEY'RE LIKE

Maine coons are smart and kind cats. They have a friendly and gentle nature. And, they get along well with children and other pets.

Unlike most **domestic cats**, this **breed** does not mind being in water. In fact, many Maine coons enjoy playing in it!

This breed's coat is nearly waterproof. That means that very little water can soak through the thick coat.

COAT AND COLOR

Cats in this **breed** can have more than 75 different color and pattern combinations. However, most are brown **tabbies**. The fur is longer on the cats' stomachs, necks, and legs. This long fur keeps them warm while lying in the snow.

Maine coons have long tufts of hair sticking out of their ears.

SIZE

Over hundreds of years, Maine coons have grown to become sturdy working cats. These cats weigh 15 to 25 pounds (7 to 11 kg). They stand 10 to 16 inches (25 to 41 cm) tall. The females are somewhat smaller.

Did you know?

As its name suggests, a Maine coon has a thick tail like a raccoon.

A Maine coon held the Guinness World Record for longest domestic cat. Stewie was almost 47 inches (120 cm) long.

FEEDING

Healthy cat food includes beef, chicken, or fish. A good name-brand food will provide the **nutrients** a cat needs.

Cat food can be dry, semimoist, or canned. Food labels will show how much and how often to feed a cat.

Cats enjoy drinking fresh water, especially from the faucet.

CARE

The Maine coon's coat only needs **grooming** if it gets tangled. They clean themselves regularly, so they rarely need baths. They should have their claws trimmed every ten to 14 days.

Maine coons are very vocal. They have high-pitched chirps and trills. They make these noises when they want food or attention.

Maine coon cats need a good veterinarian. The vet can provide health exams and **vaccines**. He or she can also **spay** or **neuter** cats.

Kittens need to see the vet several times during their first few months. Adult cats should visit the vet once a year for a checkup.

Did you know?
Most of a cat's sweat glands are in the pads on its paws.

Vets can use a stethoscope to listen to a cat's heart and lungs.

Cats have an **instinct** to bury their waste. So, cats should use a **litter box**. Waste should be removed from the box daily.

A cat buries its waste to mark its area. If a cat goes outdoors, it will begin to do the same. A **microchip** can help bring a cat home if it gets lost.

Did you know?
Cats touch their noses together as a greeting.

Cats enjoy spending time on perches. Up high, they can easily see what is happening across a room.

KITTENS

A Maine coon mother is **pregnant** for 63 to 65 days. Then, she gives birth to a **litter** of about four kittens. For the first two weeks, kittens mostly eat and sleep.

All kittens are born blind and deaf. After two weeks, they can see and hear. At three weeks, the kittens begin taking their first steps.

Young kittens cannot control their body temperature. They depend on others to keep them warm.

THINGS THEY NEED

Between 12 and 16 weeks old, Maine coon kittens are ready for **adoption**. Kittens like to be active. So, they need daily exercise. A Maine coon cat will be a loving companion for about 15 years.

Some people have trained their cats to walk on a leash.

adoption the process of taking responsibility for a pet.

breed a group of animals sharing the same appearance and features. To breed is to produce animals by mating.

Cat Fanciers' Association established in 1906, it is the world's largest registry for pedigreed cats.

domestic cats tame cats that make great pets.

Felidae the scientific Latin name for the cat family. Members of this family are called felines. They include domestic cats, lions, tigers, lynx, and cheetahs.

groom to clean and care for.

instinct a way of behaving, thinking, or feeling that is not learned, but natural.

litter all of the kittens born at one time to a mother cat.

litter box a place for house cats to leave their waste.

microchip an electronic circuit placed under an animal's skin. A microchip contains identifying information that can be read by a scanner.

neuter (NOO-tuhr) to remove a male animal's reproductive glands.

nutrient (NOO-tree-uhnt) something found in food that living beings take in to live and grow.

pregnant having one or more babies growing within the body.

spay to remove a female animal's reproductive organs.

species (SPEE-sheez) living things that are very much alike.

tabby a domestic cat with a striped and spotted coat.

vaccine (vak-SEEN) a shot given to prevent illness or disease.

Viking one of the Scandinavians who raided or invaded the coasts of Europe from the 700s to the 900s.

ONLINE RESOURCES

Booklinks
NONFICTION NETWORK
FREE! ONLINE NONFICTION RESOURCES

To learn more about Maine coon cats, visit **abdobooklinks.com**. These links are routinely monitored and updated to provide the most current information available.

INDEX